GOD'S LOVE IS MERCY

God's Love Is Mercy

Thoughts on Confession

CHRISTOPHER LOPEZ

LEONINE PUBLISHERS
PHOENIX, ARIZONA

The Scripture citations used in this work are taken from *The Inspirational Study Bible*, New King James Version, Max Lucado (ed.), copyright © 1995 by Word Bibles; and "Bible Hub," https://biblehub.com/.

Published by

Leonine Publishers LLC
Phoenix, Arizona
USA

ISBN-13: 978-1-942190-51-6

Library of Congress Control Number: 2019938832

10 9 8 7 6 5 4 3 2 1

Visit us online at www.leoninepublishers.com
For more information: info@leoninepublishers.com

CONTENTS

PREFACE. 1

PART I
THE PATH OF MERCY. 3

PART II
THE FATHER RUNS TOWARDS THE SON 13
(FOLLOWING THE PATH OF MERCY,
AND THE ENCOUNTER)

PART III
AT THE FOOT OF THE CROSS. 21
(UNDER CONFESSION: THE ENCOUNTER OF MERCY)

PART IV
THE LOVE AND COMPASSION OF CHRIST IS
MERCY 45
(FORGIVENESS IN THE MERCY OF CHRIST)

PART V
THE GIFTS OF THE SPIRIT 59
(CONFESSION, PENANCE, AND REPARATION)

PART VI
THE DESIRE FOR THE SALVATION OF SOULS 69
CLOSING THOUGHTS

BIBLIOGRAPHY. 77

The path towards the confessional might seem long, very long. Yet it is a path full of mercy, compassion, and love, because the Lord is there waiting to forgive us.

Christopher Lopez

PREFACE

Our life in the secular world might be a routine for most of us, a series of daily events that we follow like clockwork. If something happens or there is change, we might have a crisis or begin questioning ourselves: What am I doing? What am I missing? These questions are a wonderful start on the path to holiness. Certainly, we all find answers in many different ways, because the Lord knows our hearts and knows how to approach us, so that we might listen and follow Him in the most marvelous ways. Once we have discovered our call to holiness, then confession takes a very important place in our heart and mind, because we are able to see that we are imperfect and in great need of God's mercy.

Writing these thoughts on confession involved a lot of mediation, and I deeply believe that they come from our Lord. I see them through the eyes of a penitent who is in need of God's mercy. We all as penitents can experience the wonderful consolation and love that comes from this great sacrament.

We recently experienced an extraordinary time of grace, the Jubilee of Mercy, opened by Pope Francis (December 2015 – November 2016). During this Jubilee, we had many wonderful opportunities to experience God's mercy in different and extraordinary ways. It was also a time of profound reflection and many of the thoughts in this book will be linked to that wonderful time, which I believe was a special gift of our Lord to a world that is in need of mercy, to a world that can be cold-hearted, a world that is ignoring God's existence when it is in most need of Him.

We pray to our Blessed Mother, the Virgin Mary, who is always like a good mother, prepared to receive us in her arms and pray for us to the Almighty. We entrust ourselves to her and we entrust ourselves to our Lord's mercy. Amen.

Part I

The Path of Mercy

The path to holiness starts when we have an intimate encounter with Christ, when in the depths of our heart we know that we desire to be like Christ and to follow in His footsteps. Our relationship with the Lord begins to deepen even more; however, we begin to see our weaknesses, especially during times of trial, and in those moments, we understand our need of the ever-present mercy of God.

We see that God is mercy and His everlasting desire for the salvation of our soul is always present.

* * *

We can ask ourselves about the importance of mercy. We can see mercy through human eyes in the moment we desire to help someone who is in need. That impulse is a sign of God's mercy because it is an act that is not selfish. For example, if you pick up a glass of water to give to another person, it might seem like a small gesture, but you are helping them and this is a small work of mercy. When the Father gives us graces, sometimes they might not seem extraordinary, but they are. They remind us that

"Whoever is faithful with very little will also be faithful with much…" (Luke 16:10). These small graces allow us to walk forward towards spiritual perfection that will be achieved the moment we are one with Christ.

• • •

When we walk towards the priest for confession, we are going already on the path of mercy; however, this is not the start. The start is in our heart, during the moment when we acknowledge our sins and our need of forgiveness. Sometimes we tend to believe it is our own desire to seek the Lord's mercy, but it is also a grace from the Lord. Due to our condition of original sin, we receive the grace and the gift of wanting to be in communion with Him.

However, the path of mercy continues after confession. We must ask ourselves often: How will I work with the grace of the Lord? What is my desire? Am I willing to avoid sin as long as I can with the help of the Lord, or will I go against His will?

We can say, "I don't enjoy sin, I hate it!" But it could be the case, for example, that I like to eat a lot, and even though I am really full after dinner and I don't think I even can move, I see a piece of my favorite dessert and I stare at it. In that moment our conscious is struggling with our body whether to give into desire or give into God.

• • •

The path of mercy requires a lot of courage. It is guided by the Holy Spirit, because the obstacles to mercy can be our own selves. We might doubt God's mercy, but God's mercy is ever present, especially in moments when we are on our knees, broken because of sin, and we feel ashamed. Pope Francis wrote:

> Precisely in feeling my sinfulness, in looking at my sins, I can see and encounter God's mercy, his love, and go to him to receive forgiveness. In my own life, I have so often seen God's merciful countenance, his patience.[1]

How many times can we experience God's mercy, even after we've committed a sin? Our natural desire is to return and be again in communion with Him. Our Lord can use even our weaknesses to get us closer to Him. We must trust in Him — He who is ever patient and ever merciful.

* * *

Meditation is something we either overestimate or underestimate. We overestimate because we believe that this can only be achieved by religious, consecrated, or extraordinary people, and we underestimate because we believe it is limited to a church, monastery, or silence. Meditation can be done in many ways and is a wonderful spiritual exercise. It can teach us the

---

[1] "Homily of Pope Francis," 7 April 2013, http://w2. vatican.va/content/francesco/en.html.

beauty of the small graces that the Lord provides to us and sometimes we don't see.

Meditating over our sins and the mercy of God is part of the path of mercy. We can meditate by looking upon the cross, for the cross teaches us the importance of self-sacrifice and the infinite Love of God. The Father sacrificed His only Son out of mercy and love, so that He might save us from evil.

Through frequent meditation, we walk the path of mercy with a constant consolation of God, and we hope in Him who is love.

* * *

God is hope, and hope relies on the word of Christ. We cannot allow ourselves to be taken by fear, because fear is a trap in which we can be bound for an entire lifetime. No, hope is the answer!

We must walk in hope of mercy, walk in the hope of resurrection.

* * *

When we examine our conscience, it is like a ladder. We have to start from step one which is recognition of our need of God's mercy, our Father's mercy. Without the fact of God's mercy, analyzing and meditating on our sins would be worthless. We would never be able to achieve holiness, because we are great sinners. We are often in sin—if not great ones, small ones. That is why God's mercy plays a key role in everything. How wonderful is His mercy? How great is Him who can forgive everything?

We must never be afraid of "too much" mercy, but rather thank deeply and praise God for His graces towards us.

* * *

"…But where sin abounded, grace abounded much more" (Romans 5:20).

Sin starts from the very desire of the prohibited, the forbidden, or on a wish for an easier path. These actions shatter our relationship with God, because we open our heart to the evil one. It might seem like something small, but always it will grow. Our only hope in that moment is in the Lord, because He will rectify our path in a merciful way. Yet as a father, He will correct us in our mistakes. These beautiful corrections edify our spirit and help move us forward on our path to holiness.

That is why if we trust in God, grace will always abound more than sin, because mercy will be our hope, our eternal hope.

* * *

Avoiding sin is not something that is decided by ourselves, but by the commandments of the Lord. In our human society, we have a misconception of mercy. We believe mercy is God being understanding and allowing us to sin because He is merciful. This is not the right idea. God provides mercy to everybody, as long as there is a repentance from the sinner and a constant desire of change.

* * *

The examination of conscience is of vital importance, because we examine our souls in search of the cracks that need to be filled by the mercy of God. Even though it might be difficult to search and admit our difficulties, we should be able to be sincere with ourselves and with the Lord. Sometimes, just a review for five minutes can give us a glance at our need of the Almighty's mercy.

* * *

When we examine our soul before confession (and other moments such as before our night prayers), do it in hope for mercy. Our Lord gives you this opportunity to gain salvation. From the cross to the resurrection, it is a path of hope. Hoping in God's mercy is given to us by the Spirit. It allows us to see that even though our sins are many, the grace that comes from the Sacrifice of our Lord is more abundant, but only if we search for it. Therefore, it is vital that we turn towards our mother Mary.

The graces that Mary can give us are beyond our understanding, because Mary is full of mercy. She is the Mother of Mercy. Our mother can intercede and help us to walk forward because she is the devil's worst enemy, for God said, "… she shall crush thy head" (Genesis 3:15). She can help us meditate on our faults and give us hope, hope for her Son's mercy with the promise of her unique intercession.

* * *

Lord, even if I were perfect, without you I am nothing. Even if my body were immaculate, without you I am nothing. Even if I never knew sin, without you I would be lost. Even if my life was filled with merits, without you they would be worthless.

Lord, even if I loved my neighbor with all my soul and selfless charity, if I don't love you, it is worth very little. Lord, without your love I am nothing, without your mercy I am damned, and without your presence I am lost. Lord, if I ever doubt your teachings or your mercy, it is because of my worthlessness. That is why, Lord, fill my heart with your presence!

* * *

Mary, mother of mercy and hope, we kneel before you in our littleness to ask you to help us as our mother and queen. You know our Lord's infinite sea of mercy and His desire for our salvation. We humbly ask you to help us to meditate on the things that pass through our hearts during this day. Help us to see the moments in which we have lacked love or compassion, the moments in which we have been weak and we could have been strong, the moments in which we did not take advantage of our Lord's graces to get a bigger crown of glory in heaven. Allow us, Mary, to be humble enough to ask for forgiveness and follow your motherly example that will lead us to salvation. Let us walk in the path of hope and mercy, let us trust the Lord like you trusted Him, even on Calvary at the moment of His death, so we can resurrect with Him and enter His kingdom. Amen.

CLOSING THOUGHTS:

The means of preparing for confession is to humble the heart, to leave aside our "me," to ask for forgiveness of our weaknesses, and acknowledge our need of God's mercy so as to be able to achieve salvation. Our society now is what we can call a "good seller." Why? Because it sells sin like it's a good thing, and most people believe it. Society is quite sneaky; it wants to trick you with living in the moment and not worrying about your soul. As the Gospel says, "…for the sons of this age are shrewder in dealing with their own generation than the sons of the light" (Luke 16:8). We must deal with the world in a humble, yet cautious way.

Many people ask themselves: Why do I need confession? If I confess only with God, why would He not forgive me? Why do I have to go to a man that might be an equal or worse sinner than me?

The Lord said, "If you forgive the sins of any, they are forgiven, if you withhold forgiveness from anyone, it is withheld" (John 20:23). This passage cannot be turned around or, like many of our more "liberal" friends want to, put it into a "re-interpretation" or "new-interpretation" that says, "Jesus didn't mean it this way. It might just be that He wanted to do it in a figurative way…" It is crystal clear and yet is wonderful. We can receive forgiveness from the Lord and restore our relationship, which will grow more and more.

These thoughts should prepare us to embrace this wonderful, delicate, and beautiful sacrament, and remind us of the importance of preparation in order to embrace our merciful Father.

PART II

THE FATHER RUNS
TOWARDS THE SON

(FOLLOWING THE PATH OF MERCY,
AND THE ENCOUNTER)

The longing silence of the heart is covered by the constant attacks of loud crowds of thoughts that pass through our minds on a daily basis. These feelings and thoughts are sometimes unavoidable. If we examine our conscious, we may find that some of these thoughts have created huge sins from very little ones, and they make us prisoners of the constant desire of repeating them. The decision of going to confession is more and more evident.

The moment when we arrive at the church, we should find a quiet spot and pray. Offer the Lord our sincere desire for forgiveness, and embrace the little way to Golgotha, where our old self will die, in order to be cleaned and go out to the world with the light and purity that only our Lord Jesus Christ can give.

• • •

For many people, it is very difficult to arrive at the confessional; they come with really heavy stones (sins) and the devil does everything in his power to avoid their coming to the priest. We are approaching the encounter between our heavenly Father and us, we cannot back down. It is like when we are racing, we are in the last lap and we start feeling the weakness and tiredness in our body grow; however, we are certain that we are about to win, we simply cannot drop out, because all of our effort will go to waste.

Excuses there always are, but are you willing to waste God's graces? Let us pray to the Immaculata, our beloved mother who is the mother of graces. She will offer our desire of true penance to arrive pure to the Lord. With trust in her, we continue towards the encounter with the merciful Christ in the place of the priest.

● ● ●

Excuses and bad habits are best friends, they tag along so well and are a danger to us in many ways. If we are about to embrace the Father like the prodigal son, we cannot stop Him or excuse ourselves: "Father, I have sinned against heaven and against you. I am no longer worthy to be called your son" (Luke 15:21).

The son does not excuse himself by saying, "Father, you have to understand that I am young and I didn't know what I was doing," or, "Father, maybe I've sinned, but you know my brother has done this..." Excusing your bad habits makes it a bad habit, and it will only turn

14

us against God and will leave us in our own miserable "me." When we arrive, we have to be prepared for everything and embrace what the priest will tell us, because he speaks for the Lord and he forgives in His most Holy Name.

* * *

When we see that the Father comes to us, we must not be afraid. We must embrace Him, allow Him to clean our wounds and dress us, for we are again one with Him. The forgiveness that the Lord gives us is so incredible and far beyond our wild imagination—He is mercy. Let us always be hopeful in the Lord and allow Him to work in us.

* * *

Before the encounter of mercy, we might start having "cold feet," and this is the moment we must ask Our Lady for her intercession against the trickeries of the evil one. Because Our Lady is our hope and our greatest defender.

Our Lady has the eyes of mercy. She transmits like a transparent glass the mercy of the Father and she helps us embrace it as mother that she is to us. Through her powerful intercession and the graces she provides to her sons and daughters, we will be more confident in the mercy of our heavenly Father.

* * *

Prayer to Our Lady of Sorrows

O Mary, Mother of Mercy, allow us to see through your eyes, through thy merciful eyes. You that suffered, cried, and hoped at the foot of the cross, intercede for us, your children, we who cry "in this valley of tears." We are not worthy of you, but through your compassion, the same compassion you had for the sons of this world at the foot of the cross, move our hearts and allow the Spirit to guide us back to the house of the Father. We cry over our sins that are many, but trust in you to be at our side like a good mother, to console us and love us.

O Mary, you who are mother of sorrows, pray for us your children!

* * *

Look upon Our Lady, ask her to intercede for you in the Sacrament of Confession, allow her to strengthen your soul and give you the grace to not fall in the same sin. Our Lady knows the Lord's mercy in an extraordinary and unique way, "She was and is one with the Lord."[2] She knows the mercy of our Father, because she was made a temple, a perfect tabernacle for the Lord.

* * *

Once we have reached the confessional, we have to unfold our heart. We have hopefully prepared for this moment and it is time to unveil our hearts to the Lord. However, it is important to know two different aspects: first, if the priest knows us and he has heard your confession several times, or if he is a priest we have never confessed to. The importance of knowing the difference lies in the fact that if he knows us, there can be a certain continuity that can be important for our spiritual growth. Many people find it a bit difficult because they think that the priest will get bored with their sins or he will memorize them. He will say, "You did that again!?..."

A good confessor will be merciful, but we need to know that mercy sometimes can involve one or two scoldings to remind us that

---

[2] St. Louis de Montfort, *True Devotion to Mary*.

we must aim higher; however, it is also up to us to decide which priest we feel most comfortable with and ask the Lord to let us see who is the right confessor, one that will help us on our path of mercy that guides us to salvation.

* * *

When we feel scared of the confessional or we feel we go too often, we must remember that this sacrament is a sacrament of mercy. We are not confessing to a human being, we are confessing to the Lord; therefore, can we go as many times as we need. Remember that we do it from our heart, but we will also follow the Spirit's inspiration.

* * *

Open your heart to the Lord, open it to realize the wonder of this sacrament.

CLOSING THOUGHTS:

If yet not clear, these last thoughts remind us of the general dangers that can come during our journey and the preparations that we must take during the few moments on our way or while we wait for confession. This journey is a constant journey for many of us as Catholics, and yet there should be more who join, because we are all in need of our Lord's mercy, our Father's mercy. I can assure you that many dangers will come when we have decided to embrace this journey. Even the smallest thing could be a trait that hinders us, like laziness, not wanting to reach the priest, or embarrassment:

What if the priest thinks bad of me? Or excuses: It is because I never have time… These traits are manipulated by the devil, to postpone our journey and little by little to win our souls.

Let us pray to the Lord, so we might be able to embrace this wonderful path of mercy.

Part III

At the Foot of the Cross

(Under Confession: The Encounter of Mercy)

The most important thing in this encounter is God's mercy. We must always remember that we are seeking the mercy of our Lord through the confession and forgiveness of our weaknesses. We must never think of God like a judge who is seeking to punish our sins, but rather as a parent reaching out for his son to come back.

∗ ∗ ∗

Patience is an extraordinary gift of grace. During our confession we must entrust ourselves to mercy and patiently speak to the priest, opening our heart to the Lord who sees the secrets of our heart. Do not be afraid. Talk to him and be sincere; however, do not excuse yourself in the sense of blaming others or situations, but rather ask for forgiveness. Seek for mercy!

∗ ∗ ∗

"And because you are children, God has sent the Spirit of his Son into our hearts, crying, 'Abba! Father! '" (Galatians 4:6).

We are called by the Father into an act of reconciliation. He is so merciful. He sets this desire into our hearts without forcing it through; however, He allows still our free will to be the one to enter in the confessional. It is helpful to imagine that the priest is the glass in which we drink the "water of life," bringing mercy into our hearts.

When we think of the passion of Christ, something inside of us is moved. We feel the

sorrow and sacrifice that, even though ended with life defeating death, still our Lord had to endure. These questions can accompany us in confession: "Lord, why me? Why did you suffer for me? Why do you love me if am not worthy?"

* * *

"Jesus, have mercy on me!"

* * *

In confession, we must be humble, not like the Pharisee in the parable who comes to the temple and says, "God, I thank you that I am not like other people—robbers, evildoers, adulterers—or even like this tax collector. I fast twice a week and give a tenth of all I get" (Luke 18:11-12). What kind of attitude is this? Well do not be so surprised because we believe we are good people. We might be, but we are still in need of forgiveness in even the small details, and sometimes pride hurts the Lord more than any other sin, because we tell Him, "I do not need you, I will make it on my own." But we are weak, and no matter how long we walk we will fall and always our merciful Father will be present to receive us and hold us by the hand to take us back.

* * *

"But the tax collector stood at a distance. He would not even look up to heaven, but beat his breast and said, 'God have mercy on me, a sinner'" (Luke 18:13).

This man is really repentant of his sins and he asks for mercy. We also should repent from the heart. We have to see the face of Jesus and feel compassion. Let Him touch our soul and help us to move and improve in all of our daily faults. We have to be humble when we come to confession. Most of us believe that we know what we need and what we want to hear when we go to confession. Don't go to confession like that, otherwise there will never be any priest that will satisfy you, because you're thinking of the needs of your will rather than the needs of your soul. You have to go with an open heart and tell the Lord, "God, have mercy on me, a sinner."

⚬ ⚬ ⚬

Listen and meditate while you are at confession. Most want to "just get it over with" and they don't listen to the priest. We must listen, because he is not speaking in his own name, but he is speaking in the name of Christ.

⚬ ⚬ ⚬

When you confess, do it from the heart and not out of compromise or how people will perceive you. Confession is something to be happy about, but not to pride around. It is a time of mercy and a time of prayer. When you are warned by your conscience that you are doing something like this, follow your intuition, because it is not yours, but it is the Lord that reminds you that confession is not your desire, but His grace that works in you.

* * *

Stop feeling sorry for yourself! Rather, feel sorry about your sins which have caused wounds to the Lord, but don't stay there...move on! Have hope! Hope in the resurrection. Have hope in His forgiveness of you, because His grace through confession "has done wonders."

* * *

When we go to confession, we are like blind men in need of healing from the Lord. We must seek this healing for the soul, which will bring us hope and strength to keep on going forward.

* * *

When we sin, it is like a sickness. If we don't treat it, it will just spread more and more, turning into a condition. It could last a long time or even your entire life. If you are afraid of falling again in a particular sin, or sinful action that has turned into an addiction for the rest of your life, don't be afraid, find a confessor that is willing to help you and guide you. Through him, the Lord will work in you and maybe even heal you from that wound completely.

* * *

Following this thought, I like to think that sin has three different stages: mild, constant, and corruption. Let us think about the last one of these stages: sin is corruption. He who is corrupt loves his sickness; he has created a bond with sin. He rather enjoys it and does not want to repent. He has fallen in this "lack of hope" or love for money, power, pleasure, etc. We tend to forget our rather delicate situation as human beings: we can be exposed to sin and not fall in it, but there are many situations in which we might fall. We must always pray, especially to not fall into this "corruption circle," because it could mean the loss of our soul.

* * *

Do not judge others while you are waiting, or after confession when you are no longer in sin. How many of us judge the first person we see after confession? He is ugly, she is wearing a horrible dress, that one over there doesn't look like a good person, or she over there…, as if we were immaculate. This action can stain our soul, they are like ink. We must be aware always of these small sins. After confession, we are one with Christ.

* * *

Pray if you are waiting in line for confession. Ask for patience or humbleness, ask for someone who doesn't want to come or the innocent that die in peace. Use this great opportunity as a prayer to save souls through your example. Let the Lord inspire your thoughts.

* * *

"Whoever is faithful with very little will also be faithful with much" (Luke 16:10).

Again, there is this beautiful text that has so much to teach us and it is because many of us think big, especially during our youth. Many believe that to become a saint there must be martyrdom or an extraordinary event; however, we must start with baby steps and that is the moment we discover our need of a relationship with our Lord. In confession we are also walking huge steps towards holiness, for virtues and beautiful signs come through this mystical sacrament. Grace guides us through the "valley of tears" following the steps of the Lord, and through confession we can experience the wonderful love that our Lord wants to give us.

❄ ❄ ❄

O Lord, in this sadness of a world without hope, I cling to you. O Lord, in this time of shadows, I want to proclaim your Holy Name. O Lord, in this time in which the world ignores your presence, let me find the light in the small box in which you come down to listen to my faults. O Lord, I have sinned; however, you are there to embrace me, like a father to his son. I ask one thing only and it is to help me embrace you back always.

❄ ❄ ❄

Rules? Most of us debate in our heart, what is wrong and what is right? God gave us Ten Commandments to follow and the Church asks us to follow them, and we know in the bottom of our heart that these Commandments are the very core of our belief. But some of us fight with these rules, we are not easy to convince. We are like little kids, and even though our parents tell us not to do something, we will do it to prove them wrong. Sin is something like that; however, we are disobeying someone bigger than our "earthly parents," our Celestial Father, and being rebellious could bring a bigger consequence. We have to be patient and ask for His help, even when we feel hopeless. Have hope!

. . .

Who is our companion? Husband? Wife? Children? Friends? They can be with us but we have to let go eventually, and then we are alone. However, if the Lord is in our heart we will never be alone, even if we are the last person on earth. We have to think that He lives in us, He lives in YOU! How do you want His house to be?

. . .

A very beautiful task is to clean our house, fix it, and decorate it. However, temptation will come and it would shake the house and sin will be an eventual earthquake and destroy the inside of this house. That is why we have to let the Lord be our rock, our deep settle, and even if the house shakes nothing will perish.

. . .

Some people are very saint-like; they are very good people and they live very holy lives. However, even their houses need to be cleaned once in a while, like Mother Teresa of Calcutta, who used to confess every week. We have to try to be constant with confession, because

God's grace would flow in us and love will grow and grow, because "he who is forgiven little, loves little" (Luke 7:47).

* * *

Oh, Lord Jesus Christ, who thy passion you suffered for our sake, you who looks from the midst of your cross to this corrupted humanity, help us to become instruments of thy divine will, to be a part of thy holy cross, and embrace with love the sufferings of this world. Mary, intercede for us, especially for those who lack charity and mercy, those of us that can be cold-hearted or give ourselves but not fully. Help us to be humble and ask for forgiveness. Let this forgiveness bring warmth to our hearts and fill us with hope.

* * *

You haven't gone to confession for some time? Well, it is still not too late to go. The Lord is waiting for you, and if you go He will absolve you and you will be a part of the most awesome communion with Him, because He will be able to live in you and you will be one with Him.

* * *

Sometimes the desire for confession can be spontaneous and we haven't prepared. The Lord gives us wonderful grace—small, merciful gifts—that we have to embrace at the exact moment. Try to pray: "Lord, I am not prepared for this, however, if it is your will allow me to use this opportunity as if I were." We will realize that the presence of the Lord will guide us.

* * *

Encountering a priest can be a difficult task for some of us, especially if we know him and he also knows us. We think that his perspective of us will change, and that the next time he sees us he will think, "He's probably been doing that again…" However, I can tell you that if he is a good confessor, his perspective of you will grow. He will be able to do what most of us can't and it is to help you in the way your soul needs, because he is the only one (besides God) that has a bigger picture of what is happening in your heart.

* * *

A spiritual exercise that will make our soul grow is certainly to analyze our conversation with the priest and compare it to the previous one, not in the sense of seeing if this one is better or how "good" is your confessor doing. Rather, ask yourself: Have I said entirely the same? Have I improved? Which weakness do I want to especially work with?

This, together with prayer, will allow us to avoid routine during confession. Routine? Yes, in the sense of doing it just because "I have to do it!" We must experience love and forgiveness, not only feel forgiven, but actually acknowledge it.

* * *

Allow Mary to cry with you. Cry together for your faults, grief over them, because each sin is part of the heavy cross the Lord took upon Himself. Why would Mary join you? Because she is your mother and she knows sorrow very well; however, she will be your strength, the foundation on which you will be able to support yourself and stand up, so that you might keep on walking in the path towards holiness. Mary, as your mother, desires you to go to heaven and rejoice with the angels and the saints for all eternity.

• • •

To analyze the encounter, to find the meaning of confession, we have to go deep into the heart of God. Mercy flows without limit there and God wants us to connect in this river, but mercy cannot pass if God's word doesn't live in our hearts. Let us encounter His love, live His word in the depths of our heart.

• • •

Do some quiet time with the Lord and prepare your heart to embrace this sacrament. Prayer is the way to achieve the best confession.

• • •

When you pray and meditate before, during, and after confession, don't go around looking for prayers as if they were scientific formulas. No! Just talk to Him. He wants to listen to you, to your words. Yes, you can use one of the wonderful written prayers that the Church has given us, but talk to Him, tell Him how much you care for Him, and thank Him for how much He loves you.

* * *

Get yourself a cross! Yes, a cross, not a metaphorical one, but a real one. It can be a crucifix or just a cross, look at it while you are in confession, because then you won't be able to deny anything. The cross is a reminder of the moment in which God showed you how much He is willing to love you; how much He loves you!

* * *

> Holy men and women have tried to practice the good things which they believed and were able to do. And they have fulfilled by holy desire what they could not achieve in practice. Their holy desire made up for what was lacking in their practice. If anyone had perfect faith, he would reach a point where he would be given complete certainty. So, if your faith is good, your deeds will be good.[3]

We have to desire that change, the conversion of the heart. Brother Giles as a follower of Saint Francis learns to be humble and through this he also grows in grace, allowing himself to see that desire of God for us is to desire to be more and more united to Him. "And they

---

[3] R. Brown, trans. and ed., *The Little Flowers of Saint Francis* (Garden City, New York: Doubleday & Company, Inc., 1958), 263.

have fulfilled by holy desire what they could not achieve in practice...."[4] This can be our call from God, especially with certain crosses that, if we do not carry with patience, they can become sins. When we are ready to embrace this change, the flames of "holy desire" start to grow in ourselves; however, we must take good care of them, and even if we do not achieve to change certain aspects, we always have to have the desire to. We must let the Lord guide us through the confessor to spot these certain crosses, so that we might not only desire, but eventually achieve and be consoled by the Lord.

* * *

We must always remember that the Lord gives us crosses; these crosses are our path in the way to achieve holiness. We must not think of holy people as the only ones chosen by God, because then you are most certainly in a mistake, because we are all called to be holy men and women, that is why we can all have "the holy desire" of correcting our wrong doings and reach the point "where we could be given complete certainty" of our actions and deeds.[5] We can and should use the confessional as a place to grow in holiness, to humble ourselves and let "our burden be lightened and we will rest our souls" (Matthew 11:29).

* * *

---

[4] Ibid.
[5] Ibid.

All crosses are a gift that will lead us to Christ; they will help us grow in sanctity and holiness for salvation. The Lord will always give us crosses that we can handle, not by ourselves, but with His help and that is when we have to trust in God's grace. We can ask ourselves what Pope Francis said:

> What has the cross given to those who have gazed upon it and to those who have touched it? What has the cross left in each one of us? You see, it gives us a treasure that no one else can give: the certainty of the faithful love that God has for us. A love so great that it enters our sin and forgives it, enters into our sufferings and gives us the strength to bear it.[6]

That "faithful love" can be our strength to carry our daily cross, especially for those who are sick or live in a state of sin from which they are struggling to get out.

● ● ●

The cross is a tremendous gift and, through confession, hope can flow and we will be able to hug the cross and follow in the Lord's footsteps towards eternity.

● ● ●

We cannot ignore the fact that sexuality is more and more public and has become an open topic

---

[6] Pope Francis, *Lent with Pope Francis,* ed. Donna Giaimo (Boston, MA: Pauline Books & Media, 2014).

for our human society. What does this have to do with confession? Well very much, because this in its pure nature is not sinful; it is an act of love in which a man and woman become "one flesh" and they "know completely each other." They enter in communion with each other and their love binds them together in a way that "they are given to know each other."[7] However, this has been degraded by society to mere pleasure and no responsibility, so if you think like this, it probably is a good time for you to go to confession.

* * *

We must respect each other and respect our bodies, learn to love each other, and even if we sin, we have to confess and start again. How many people struggle with this sin? Well many of us certainly, but we have to love God and see the beauty through His eyes, not through the eyes of men that feed our imagination with different fantasies that will just bring sadness and loneliness to our life. We must learn to confess this sin with patience and courage, because it is difficult to reveal this intimate part of our life, that probably only ourselves, the priest, and God will ever truly know.

* * *

Do not be discouraged, have hope! We have to have hope! This beautiful feeling that is

---

7 "General Audiences: John Paul II's Theology of the Body," (1980), https://www.ewtn.com/library/PAPALDOC/JP2TBIND.HTM.

inspired by the Holy Spirit is key for our way in the confessional. We have to understand that without hope there is no place for God in our heart. Why? Because achieving repentance will take us as far as the confessional, but what after? That is what we have to have present when we go to confession. Where is the Lord taking me? What is His will for me?

* * *

The *Catechism* of our Holy Mother Church says:

> Those who approach the sacrament of Penance obtain pardon from God's mercy for the offense committed against Him, and are, at the same time, reconciled with the Church which they have wounded by their sins and which by charity, by example, and by prayer labors for their confession (*Catechism of the Catholic Church*, no. 1422).

Our sins have consequences and real consequences that can affect not only our relationship with the Lord, but also with the Church. It is fine to question and discuss matters of faith; however, it is one thing to discuss them and another one is to doubt them, judge them, or even attack them. We can "wound the Church" with our actions, because as believers we are members of the body that is our Holy Mother Church and that constantly is working to help to save our soul. Our task is to avoid sin, but if we fail and we confess, we are recognizing our mistake and our need of Christ the Lord, and

His Church that administrates this wonderful Sacrament of Penance.

* * *

Following the previous thought, "Those who approach the Sacrament of Penance obtain pardon from God's mercy for the offense committed against Him..."

When we approach the confessionary, we receive God's mercy. As Mother Angelica once said, "You don't need to feel forgiven, you are forgiven!"[8] We cannot base the wonderful mercy of forgiveness from the Lord on our mere simple feelings, because if we based it on feelings, then the Ten Commandments or teachings of the Church wouldn't make sense. You are one with Christ and the Church after confession, you are forgiven. Isn't it wonderful? God is willing to forgive and forget... just like that, and He does it because HE LOVES YOU! And He wants you to approach Him as the Father of Mercy and not as the "Cosmic God."[9]

* * *

---

[8] "A Few Thoughts: Go to Confession," Mother Angelica Live Classics, published on 9 August 2011, accessed 10 April 2017, https://www.youtube.com/watch?v=-o4O-_TqgWk.

[9] "El Papa: Oración no es magia y no rezamos a un 'Dios cósmico' sino a un Padre cercano," Aciprensa, published on 20 June 2013, accessed 11 April 2017, https://www.aciprensa.com/noticias/el-papa-oracion-no-es-magia-y-no-rezamos-a-un-dios-cosmico-sino-a-un-padre-cercano-82149/.

When we want strength and courage to avoid sin, let us have recourse to the Immaculata and pray for her motherly protection, which is key on our way to confession, during confession, and in our new life after confession. *"Omnia possum in Eo, qui me per Immaculate confortat"* (I can do all things in Him, who strengthens me through the Immaculata), wrote Saint Maximilian around 1934.[10] Through Mary we can be comforted, and we will find a mother who is willing to guide us on a new path, a path that is connected and it is the path towards our Lord Jesus Christ. Mary is one with Him and He is one with Her. Through Her chastity we can find rest and strength to keep up with the journey.

* * *

When we wait to confess a mortal sin, it is like playing with death. Why? Because your soul is hanging from a delicate thread and if you wait for the last minute, you might not make it. You are not risking your life here, which is a temporal one, but you are risking your eternity in the flames. We have to be constant in confession, especially with mortal sin, because how can you live calmly when you have insulted and hurt the Almighty God.

* * *

---

[10] Hilda Brown, *She Shall Crush Thy Head: Selected Writings of St. Maximilian Kolbe* (Phoenix, Arizona: Leonine Publishers), 43.

If we believe in ourselves as sinners there is room for mercy; however, we have to believe in this mercy. It is not valid to only believe in the punishment. Those who believe in their hearts that there is no salvation, but keep on praying for mercy without believing and teach other people these same wrongdoings, are liars. They are liars because they believe only halfway, they do not seek for mercy, they do not believe in mercy, and they call God a liar. Why? "Blessed are the merciful, for they shall obtain mercy..." (Matthew 5:7). This is one of the many passages that speak of mercy. Now these people are not merciful, they deny mercy to their brothers and sisters. Now be aware of these people and pray for them, pray so that they will encounter the merciful Father in their hearts.

* * *

Confession is a beautiful way to open your heart, especially if you have been away from the Church. Your heart will be opened to Christ, to the Almighty. This opportunity will be unique and if it's authentic, it will be marvelous because a good confession is the start of the marathon, the marathon to heaven. Yes! A marathon to heaven! Why? Because you start the journey of mercy and with every confession, you will grow in holiness.

If you haven't been to church for some time now, "Do not be afraid...," because "you have found favor with God...."(Luke 1:30). How can this salutation to the blessed Mary relate to us? Well, if God revealed to you in your heart that you needed to go to confession, it was because you found favor in His eyes and He is telling you to come back to Him, the most Merciful. Let us pray to the Blessed Mother for guidance, especial for those souls who wish to come back, but are uncertain or are in need of guidance.

* * *

Sometimes when we are in confession and even after confession, when we are in prayer, we should ask God "for a big heart."[11] A heart "that can forgive and forget, because God has forgiven and forgotten my sins."[12] How many of us are in the confessional and expect forgiveness, but we cannot forgive our brother? We have to ask for a "big heart," because otherwise we might encounter difficulties in our spiritual life and we will become selfish, because we are willing to take, but not to give mercy and we will have to pay for our debts and for our lack of mercy.

* * *

When one lives the path of mercy, mercy cannot only be lived with other people, but also inside ourselves. It is something that has to be born from the heart of one's self. It is difficult to be merciful with one's self. Why? Many will

---

[11] Pope Francis, *Lent with Pope Francis,* ed. Donna Giaimo (Boston, MA: Pauline Books & Media, 2014), p. 69.
[12] Ibid.

think it is self-indulgence, but when we sin, we allow ourselves to be deep in this sea of despair and doubts. Even if we are living the way to holiness, we are still simple human beings and we cannot go alone in this way; this is where the "Father" gets involved in a more personal way. We cannot be afraid of our sins or thoughts, because if we give them our fear, we are just feeding the devil and strengthening him. He will attack even more. We have to use hope as a weapon of Christ, remembering that He is the one we want to follow and lead our lives.

* * *

There are so many people these days that live with the idea of "me, me, and me." Even when they go to confession, they self-pity themselves and they seek for mercy, but they are selfish people; they are willing to sacrifice others in order to live a "good Spiritual life." An example would be two kids who are playing and they fall into a pile of mud. Well one of them is more agile than the other and tells him, "Come, I will stand on you so I can get out." He gets out and then he lives, saying, "Oh, how dirty am I, I better clean myself up." You see he abandons his neighbor, because he is to "self-focused." We cannot use other people as excuses or take advantage of them, because then we are not going the right way. We cannot give up on anyone, even if just in prayer.

* * *

Gaze on Mary's eyes, through them there is an insight of God's mercy. Why? Mary's eyes are connected to her heart, a pure and immaculate heart, which gives us hope for us "poor sinners."[13]

* * *

We have to believe in the need of conversion. The saints through God's grace have asked us to follow conversion as a long-life journey in the mercy of God, a journey that is continuous within the path of mercy, because sin is ever-present, but mercy everlasting. Following the path of mercy is something wonderful and unique, something which we are in very much need today.

* * *

According to Saint Ignatius, there are two ways to fall into mortal sin. On the first one, we consent to the temptation and we act upon it, committing in that moment a mortal sin. The second one is when one acts upon it for a longer period of time, repeats it constantly, and has no intention of changing, because he is "comfortable."[14]

Mortal sin is a stone on the path of mercy and it depends on us and the acting grace of God to discern the way we are going to work

---

[13] Sister Lucia of Fatima, *Memorias de la Hermana Lucia,* 14th edition, ed. Louis Kondor (Fátima: Fundação Francisco e Jacinta Marto, 2016).

[14] Ignatius of Loyola, *Ejercicios Espirituales* (Santander: Editorial Sal Terrae, 2013), 12.

with it. Constant prayer is required, but we can also ask our Blessed Mother to help us. These sins, depending on which state we are in, will require mercy, love, compromise, and prayer.

* * *

The sins of the flesh are sins that in many people can become a constant state of sin, because ever since man became man and allowed mortal sin into this world, he has made this "act of love" to seem something corrupted, dirty, or an "animal state" of some sort. People think of the flesh as "a need, an urge to do," and chastity is something that cannot be included in the picture. We are not animals. We need to learn that love goes beyond that and when one acknowledges this in confession, he is loving God, he is recognizing that he wants to search for love rather than merely "pleasure." We have to learn to love and respect ourselves, but most of all, learn to love God.

* * *

Confession "is the movement of a contrite heart, drawn and moved by grace to respond to the merciful love of God who loved us first" (CCC, no. 1428). To respond to this call is an extraordinary grace, because this reconciles us both with God and with the Holy Catholic Church. We need confession, because we acknowledge then the need of God, the need of His forgiveness and His marvelous mercy.

CLOSING THOUGHTS:

Under confession, more happens than what meets the eye, for it is the actual fight to sanctity, and the appreciation of the opportunity to be forgiven by the sacrifice that Christ made on the cross. Sometimes for us it can be just a split second, a split second that will repeat itself weekly, monthly, or yearly. For others it doesn't even happen, but that split second is maybe the only moment in which a person will encounter mercy, understanding, and forgiveness. The world today is looking for mercy, for forgiveness. They want to sell us freedom as libertinism; however, true freedom is love and an open soul, an open soul to the love and mercy of Christ.

PART IV

THE LOVE AND COMPASSION OF CHRIST IS MERCY

(FORGIVENESS IN THE MERCY OF CHRIST)

Mercy flows from God as a grace to us, so we can be in constant communion with Him "because even if we have received the new life in Christ, it has not abolished the frailty and weakness of human nature" (CCC, no. 1426). We live in the grace of the Lord; however, we are still weak human beings. Like a house, even if we clean it, eventually if we don't take care of the house, dust will come and little by little will corrupt our soul. That is why we should try to confess often, live in the mercy of Christ, in this new life that has been given to us through our baptism.

* * *

When you go to confession, don't go saying, "I am going, but I know that God will hold my sins against me until after judgment day." Believe me, there are people that might think in this way; however, God is all goodness, He does not hold anything after confession, because you are forgiven. It is not a temporal forgiveness or like anesthesia for your conscience. No! It is real forgiveness; however, when you think about the judgment after you leave this world, ask for God's mercy. Hope in that mercy, because God is not waiting to punish you, but to receive you in His arms.

* * *

God has called us to conversation since the beginning of time, when our first parents sinned against Him through original sin, and He followed through until the prophets, and they preached, asked for conversion from the heart, and not just a "mental forgiveness" or an "exchange-conversion," like it was through sacrificing animals and then you were good to come Home. This desire of God to give mercy, led Him to send His only Son to redeem us, and He also preached and asked for a thorough conversion, a conversion from the heart.

We have to live the Sacrament of Confession, we have to breath it, to avoid an "exchange-conversion" situation, "I confess because then God is ok with me and I am ok with Him." Confession is not a transaction, it is a need of acknowledging to God that we want to live "in the mercy of Christ" and as one with Him.

* * *

Mother Angelica said: "He says he will not confess his sins to a man—to another sinner like Himself. But is this true? How many people, friends and strangers, already see his sins? People he has confided in, neighbors and relatives see his weaknesses. His family often suffer from those weaknesses."[15] Most people never think of these small details. They don't want to confess to a sinner, but most of the people that really know him, they are aware of his weaknesses or eventually they become aware of them.

When we have done something wrong, there is one difficult task and one easy solution according to the world: ask for forgiveness, but excuse yourself, because even if you did something wrong, somebody else had part of the blame for your actions. "Oh, I apologize I crashed your car, but you know, next time you should park a bit more to the right or you know don't park at all, because then I will have more space." Excuses and more excuses, these excuses in confession are excuses that God does not need to hear.

* * *

Following the previous thought, people come with the excuse: "Oh, I don't confess with this priest, because I know Him, and oh... he drinks and does this and that..." Well, first that is gossip and second you are excusing yourself on another's man weaknesses, just to avoid confession. The priest is only an intercessor from

---

[15] Mother Angelica, "Why Do You Stay Away?" (EWTN, 1999), https://www.ewtn.com/library/mother/ma53.htm.

Christ, to be able to absolve you and forgive you from your sins.

* * *

Christ's love for you is so filled with mercy that He will forgive you as many times as needed, but as long as there is a conversion and a purpose of not committing the sin again. When you have that inner desire, that desire of conversion after you've sin, you shouldn't run away from it, you should think, "I just sinned and now I want to be with God." That is a sign of mercy, a sign of His love for you! Embrace this, apologize to God from the depth of your heart in the moment, pray from your heart, tell Him how sorry you are. Then when you are able to confess, just confess and propose to God, the desire of not doing it again. This is a part of the long-life journey of mercy.

* * *

If only my heart could be one with your love and mercy, God, if only my soul could live in your heart. If only my actions could always be guided by your spirit, if only sin didn't blind my judgment. Lord, have mercy on me!

* * *

Sometimes we have to understand that sin is not only judged on a human level, but it has consequences on the spiritual level. Every time you sin, you reject God. This is sad, but true, and it hurts the Holy Heart of Jesus, especially because He is ever merciful. Let us think, How many times have I rejected God? How many times have I said: "God I don't need you?" Think quietly and find the answer in your heart, because then you will see how merciful can God be and will be just for you!

* * *

When you meet Jesus in your heart, when you truly use time to meditate and acknowledge His presence in your heart, this is the key moment of true mercy. Mercy is not an ideology or a specific right: "Oh, I have the right of mercy." No mercy is much more than any of these things, because you cannot force a person to be merciful to you. You can ask or beg for mercy; however, it is up to the judge or person at hand, but the mercy that God is giving you, surpasses every kind of human mercy. This mercy can be obtained by anyone and is ever existing, but with the only condition of a true conversion.

* * *

Christ said in a parable that the kingdom of heaven is like a grain of mustard seed (Matthew 13:31), and I believe this grain of mustard is mercy. Why? Because the kingdom of God is mercy. It is a path that is directly guided by God in our hearts, through the grace that falls from the Holy Heart of Jesus to our soul. This seed of mercy is the one that grows until it "becomes the greatest among herbs, and becomes a tree..." (Matthew 13:32). Mercy is the one that helps us grow in holiness, towards the kingdom of God. Why? Through confession we receive the grace of pardon of our sins, which makes us grow in humility, but it also creates a continuous sincerity of our hearts with Christ.

* * *

When Christ was on the cross, He had upon Himself all the sins of the world. How many sins do we carry upon us? How many sorrows? How many secrets? Might not only be ourselves, but also somebody else, somebody we know, that is struggling. Secrets in the depth of our heart, which we believe that nobody has access to; however, I am sorry to say, but God and the devil have access to them. The devil is always in the acting and he will take any opportunity to use this against you, for you to lie or back talk about this person.

The same if it is a "personal secret." We have to carry these crosses every day; however, we do not need to carry them alone, but rather allow a confessor to guide us in the love of Christ. The importance of this is to seek comprehension and moral guidance, seek for mercy, reach out your hand to the Lord.

* * *

What should scare us most in these days are the "passive souls." Passive souls? Yes, they are passive, because they can leave with Mass, but also without Mass, with confession once every year and communion every now and then, maybe. These people are Catholics "a la minute," they can be in Church one second and at the other one, they are gone. They don't care about mercy, they do not live mercy. Analyze how do you live your faith, but most importantly in which place is the need of mercy, because if you don't find it, then there is something wrong going on there. That is where forgiveness in the mercy of Christ has to occur. Ask the Lord to give you that need of conversion in your heart, that true spirit of forgiveness and prayer.

* * *

O Lord Jesus, let me reach out to your mercy, allow my heart to be a part of yours. Allow me to ask for true forgiveness from the bottom of my heart. I ask mercy for all of those who are resentful, for those who do not seek mercy, but in their unhappiness, make others miserable. Lord touch their hearts with a tiny flame of your Sacred Heart, so that they might not resist the happiness that your love can bring them. Allow them, Lord, if it's your will to know mercy, allow us to know mercy!

* * *

"Come to me, all you who labor and are overburdened, and I will give you rest" (Matthew 11:23).

Rest in the merciful arms of God, let His mercy fill your heart. The world moves like a clock, it keeps on ticking and you cannot stop it, it just keeps on going with or without you.

However, God is ever present, even when you are not always present, God lives in you. Many of us can say that we do not dedicate enough time to God or we don't live very often to serve, but rather be served, but sometimes we have to set aside our selfishness or lack of time and rest in God's merciful arms. Through Christ, through the Blessed Sacrament can we give ourselves more and more to Him.

● ● ●

Keep in mind these thoughts, because we all are in need of rest from the world, even people that live the consecrated life. This is why we have retreats, and why an extraordinary time is given to recognize ourselves unworthy of the mercy of God, and to renew our willingness on striving to Him in it, rather than just live in penance. What do I mean by life in penance? Penance is healthy and it helps us to purify our soul; however, if we only live in a constant penance, we will never be able to love other virtues and "enjoy" the graces that come with them.

Thinking about a glass again, we wash a glass to use it and when it is dirty we wash it, then if we want to give it a special touch, we polish it a bit. However, we cannot live polishing the glass our entire time, because then when is it going to receive the "water of life"?

● ● ●

"Blessed be the endearing love of Christ, that moved by piety for my misery, offers me all the ways to reach His love!"[16] This phrase of Saint Gemma Galgani can express the desire of the heart for our Lord, for Him to be reached, for Him to be loved, and for Him to be welcomed in our own hearts. He is the way in which we have to walk; however, He sets paths for everyone to reach their goal, which is Him. Not everybody can drive on the highway, some people have to start on a difficult road, but with perseverance they can reach the highway, they can reach the love of Christ.

* * *

---

[16] J. Solano, *Desarrollo Histórico de la Reparación en el culto al Corazón de Jesús* (Roma: Centro Cuore di Cristo, 1980).

Do you see this wonderful painting? This is Jesus that comes to you. He is ready to embrace you. You can see His wounded, but open Heart for you. Whenever you go to confession take this image with you, if not physically save it in your heart, then remember it in the moment that confession is about to start because that's the compassion and mercy that you are receiving, an open heart which is willing to receive yours and forgive you out of love.

• • •

We receive the merits of Christ, which are divine merits and these merits hold us after confession. This is "forgiveness in the mercy of Christ." Because the Lord allows His merits to flow again in you in a full way, it is like your fuel that you need to keep on fighting. These merits make us worthy of Him, not our own, but His merits that clothe us in love and mercy.

● ● ●

Christ, have mercy on me, your unworthy servant!

● ● ●

Saint Mary Magdalene of Pazzi had a vision:

> The great goodness of God is like a big river, in which there is huge and beautiful fish, so I understood that they were the souls of the blessed and saints in paradise, which they do like fish at sea, they submerge and feed themselves from the great goodness of God.

We have to allow ourselves to swim in this beautiful river, because the goodness of God is without measure and it becomes a life figure in Christ, whose true compassion and mercy brought Him to sacrifice Himself for us in the most difficult of ways. Can you sacrifice yourself a little through confession?

● ● ●

After confession, we have to start living again the Christ-like life. We must surrender ourselves to His goodness and allow Him to guide the ship to safe harbor. This ship is our life and the harbor is paradise, but the only way to allow ourselves is through prayer and through sacrifice, and to avoid sin but not by disguise, such as, "I am not going to eat because I am on a diet… Oh, but it's all for you, Lord!" Of course, you can offer your diet, but then you are gaining something and then the "sacrifice" is not only for Him anymore, it loses a bit of its autonomy. When you sacrifice something, even if it's small and you believe is meaningless, just offer it to our Lord and I promise it won't go by unnoticed.

* * *

The merits of our Lord Jesus Christ are the ones that allow us to fight the battle against sin. That is why it is important to allow Him to walk by our side and not tell Him, "Jesus, I can on my own!" Because then you are allowing yourself to give into pride. Confession is a sacrament in which we tell Jesus: "I need you! Please, I don't want to be trapped, I want to fly towards you and be free. I want to love you, Jesus!" Pride is not an option, but humbleness is required. All of this is possible through one path, and it is through the compassion of Jesus for us.

* * *

"Then Jesus answered: Woman, you have great faith! Your requested is granted" (Matthew 15:27).

In this episode, we can observe one of the multiple acts of mercy that Jesus does;

however, there is something particular and it is the other person. The Canaanite woman was out of place in the scene. Why? Because she was well aware of who Jesus was and that He had come for the salvation of Israel; however, she allows her faith to guide her through the difficult path. Do we allow ourselves to be this way? Are we willing to persevere in our faith? Are we willing to ask for forgiveness as much as it is required? Are we willing to ask God to help with the sins and things that are the most difficult for us?

* * *

CLOSING THOUGHTS:

The love of Christ is mercy. Ask Jesus that He give us a great heart, one that is willing to love and sacrifice its pride The heart that truly loves, allows to be forgiven. Sometimes we just have to allow Christ to open our heart, to give meaning to our wrongdoings. We need to sanctify ourselves through Him so that we might be able to love Him forever. We believe that we search for the love and mercy of Christ, but it is actually Christ who is calling us to love Him, to ask for forgiveness, and to rest in His mercy. Allow Jesus to be compassionate with you, allow Him in your life.

PART V

THE GIFTS OF THE SPIRIT

(CONFESSION, PENANCE, AND REPARATION)

The Holy Spirit is our guide. He can help us through His holy inspiration in a way that we might be able to remember the sins that are in our heart.

Through a litany or a short mental prayer, we can include Him in our confession and ask Him to help us to remember what He desires us to confess, so as not to forget any sin, not even a venial sin. Allow the Spirit to come to you!

* * *

O Holy Spirit, I desire your inspiration and mercy, you that have inspired saints and holy people. I ask you to inspire me, especially because now I want to ask for God's pardon and mercy. Take over my spirit in a way that I might be able to appreciate, live, and venerate this moment of mercy that you, with the Father and the Son in your infinite love have granted me. Allow me to remember this love under the sacrament and to live the sacrament, to carry it on in the mercy I show to others.

● ● ●

"Everything else matters so little except for offending the good God."[17]

This phrase from Saint Maravillas, a Carmelite nun from Madrid, is truly a remarkable phrase and it reminds us of the love of God. We have to remember that offending Him is offending the omnipotent God. The good God is so merciful that He allows us to live in freedom and He tolerates our mistakes. How many of us cannot forgive after a person we know does something against us? We have to ask the Holy Spirit to remind us of this phrase and let the meaning of the phrase be imbedded in our heart. Because where there is love, there is always a renewal of faith and always a new opportunity for mercy.

● ● ●

Inspiration of a true conversion can only come from the Holy Spirit; however, we can always ask for mercy and grace, in a way that all our confessions might be "true conversions."

● ● ●

Through the eyes of the Holy Spirit we can ask for mercy, because He can help us to go into a deeper meditation. One can always remember the merits of the passion, the sorrows and the pain that our beloved Jesus Christ suffered

---

[17] Santa Maravillas de Jesús, *Pensamientos Maravillas de Jesús* (Èditions du Signe, 2002).

for us on the cross. Because it is through His merits that we are able to receive forgiveness and increase our inner desire of God. Always remember the passion, a thorough act that opened the doors of mercy.

● ● ●

"Beloved Jesus Christ, I commend to thy divine heart my actions so as to purify and complete them."[18]

This phrase from a prayer of Saint Peter Canisius can allow us to start thinking about absolution and penance. After confession, we often think, "It's over," or "Finally…," and some of us forget to do our penance, or we are sloppy in it. I am not thinking of the consequences in the sense of rules that our Catholic Church has for not doing the penance, but the actual impact in our personal prayer life. Why? When we have offended the good God, don't we want to do something for Him? Something to regain His trust and thank Him for His mercy? When we apologize to someone, we often try to make it up to them. Why not do the same for God? We have to ask the Spirit to inspire us to do our penance in a way in which we "make it up" to God, but not out of fear, but out of love.

● ● ●

---

[18] J. Solano, *Desarrollo Histórico de la Reparación en el culto al Corazón de Jesús* (Roma: Centro Cuore di Cristo, 1980).

Penance is a sign of repentance, but is also a glass of fresh water for the soul. It allows us to give strength to fight against the dangers and the next temptations that might be already acting on our minds, after the exercise of confession. Even if the penance is small, it is a sign of mercy and an opportunity to show your inner desire of a life without sin for Jesus, who loves you and desires your salvation.

● ● ●

Sometimes you might think that your penance is too small, but you might experience it to be more difficult to do at other times, because of the fact of it being a penance. The Holy Spirit allows it to be difficult, but He also inspires us to be able to make it and work through it. We have to offer all our penances as our way to sanctification, but also as a way of asking for a "deeper" forgiveness from Jesus.

● ● ●

Dear confessors, let the Holy Spirit guide you, allow Him to lead the way into a deeper meaning of the confession. The Spirit will guide your words, so that you might be able to guide the soul who is at your feet, who is asking for mercy. Don't doubt, but guide the soul of the sinner, because he is there to ask for forgiveness. The Holy Spirit will be your guidance for the soul.

● ● ●

In penance, a good confessor must be merciful, but just. He doesn't give just any kind of penance, but tries to find one that can actually "help the soul." He believes that this penance will allow the soul to grow. Know that the Holy Spirit guides your soul to humble herself in front of the priest, who hears your confession in the person of our Lord Jesus Christ.

* * *

We live in a time when penance is no longer acceptable. We think we must not suffer, because if you want to live the "ideal life," you have to be always at "comfort." But we acknowledge that we don't live "an ideal life," because there is sin and we always have to be aware of it. Confessing is a part, but doing penance is the other part. You can say that penance is "true love." Why? Because penance allows our spirit to grow, it allows us to seal our "fight" against sin in the love of Christ, and finally it allows us to restore our damaged relationship with Christ.

* * *

Penance is not only about suffering, it is about loving. Many people think of the word "penance" and they think of a person "punishing" himself, but penance is not about "punishing" yourself. It is an act of true charity, an act of love to God, and it is a way to restore balance in our soul. Sometimes the love we put in things can be more important than the act itself.

* * *

We are in need of much mercy, but not pettiness, because many people think that we are called to accept people's mistakes (or sins). Sometimes mercy can actually be to give correction and stand for our faith, and not allow mistakes to be a constant and acceptable reality. Sin is sin, whenever and wherever. The moment when there is no more sin, that is when you are united with God, think of that. Wow! His omnipresence and His love, all very alive and very close. You will be one with Him. No more suffering, giving eternal praise to Jesus, with the Blessed Mother, and all the angels and saints. That is why you have to really live under the Spirit's guidance, so that you may be an instrument of mercy.

* * *

Understanding is not the same as accepting. We are called to understand people, to help people. Many people think that mercy is accepting certain sins, because they are circumstantial or they seem unavoidable; however, sin is sin. We have to act in a merciful way to others, by listening to them, by showing them and allowing the Spirit to guide them. The Holy Spirit would always inspire us to follow after the path of Christ, to find that everlasting mercy and the correct way to improve that which will lead us to eternal life.

* * *

Until when, O Lord, will all sinners love you; until when will they realize your eternal mercy is for them to receive; until when will they be able to allow themselves to be guided by your holy hand?

* * *

"O how difficult it is to see the earthly things, which are not God, but it makes me suffer even more, that many people go after them."[19]

Our penance after confession, if it's well guided by the Spirit, can actually be offered as well for an intention. Sometimes a penance can be the gateway to avoid one particular sin as well. We have to allow the Spirit to guide us, so all our penances can become a crown of glory. Many people think that if the priest asks us to pray an Our Father, it is too simple. Well, I have a solution for you, pray one Our Father not only then, but also in every temptation of that particular sin that is most difficult for you to handle. No longer so easy, right? Well if you want to add just a tiny bit more, offer it all for a particular intention or put it in the hands of our Blessed Mother, the Virgin Mary.

* * *

"Reparation" comes from the term "repair, make up for" and it has a certain importance, because it can be the next step in confession.[20] It can help us with our "true repentance." You can wonder why "reparation," comes after

---

[19] Santa Maravillas de Jesús, *Pensamientos Maravillas de Jesús* (Èditions du Signe, 2002).

[20] J. Solano, *Desarrollo Histórico de la Reparación en el culto al Corazón de Jesús* (Roma: Centro Cuore di Cristo, 1980).

penance when you've already confessed your sins and that is very true; however, "reparation" can help us repair our relationship in a deeper and constant way. It can as well be our way to offer our temptations and actions for all souls that, like us, are sinners, but they don't want to repent and they keep on damaging their inner connection with God.

· · ·

When we think about "reparation," it does not mean complicated actions or hours in prayer. We can make amends by extending the mercy of Christ to our neighbor, by being patient, caring, and merciful. We must forgive in the way that Jesus asks us to forgive, "seventy-seven times" (Matthew 18:22), and learn to "forget" in the sense of a constant love for that person that harmed us. For example, if a person that we go to work with makes a big mistake and blames us for it, after everything is solved, we may have a different perspective of this person, but we cannot seek revenge, even if it is our first instinct. We have to keep on going to work with this person, so we keep on asking Jesus for help in a way that He helps us to keep on forgiving this person, even though we still remember his wrong-doings. It is a Christ-like mercy and it allows us to walk towards the kingdom, in a loving way.

· · ·

Love, love, and love will allow us to live confession. When you love Christ, there is the fullness of mercy. This allows you to stand up and keep moving forward on the path of mercy, on the path of life. Love Jesus!

* * *

CLOSING THOUGHTS:

Confession is a constant situation, even for those who are closest to God, because it's not pride that guides them, it is true humility. This humility can only be given by Christ. We may feel that we don't want to humble ourselves, because it's not "natural," or because we are proud and we want to be right. Accepting that we did wrong is our desire to embrace Him, to embrace Him at the cross, in those open arms which desire us! Christ came to suffer for us "out of love." Don't you want to offer your everyday sufferings or problems? Don't you want to love Him more? Pray to the Holy Spirit, so that in confession you can see that profoundness, that love, that sacrifice, and that desire of the Spirit for the salvation of your soul. Jesus wants to save your soul! Don't you want to love Him, who has loved you, and will love you forever?

Part VI

The Desire for the Salvation of Souls

Closing Thoughts

"Therefore, do not fear them. For there is nothing covered that will not be revealed, and hidden that will not be known. Whatever I tell you in the dark, speak in the light; and what you hear in the ear, preach on the housetops. And do not fear those who kill the body, but cannot kill the soul. But rather fear Him who is able to destroy both soul and body in hell. Are not two sparrows sold for a copper coin? And not one of them falls to the ground apart from your Father's will. But the very hairs of your head are all numbered. Do not fear therefore; you are of more value than many sparrows" (Matthew 10:26-31).

How many times do we fear those who can "kill the body," and we do not accept our call to preach about mercy, to preach the love of Christ, because we are afraid of "our pride" being "killed" or being "killed" by rejection. We have to desire the salvation of our soul, but also of our brothers and sisters, of our sons and

69

daughters, our fathers and mothers. Preach God's mercy, invite people through prayer, invite people through example, use all methods for the conversion of souls. How many of these thoughts I wish could bring you that desire, that love for souls and an open heart for the confessional!

• • •

"Love Him, love my Jesus, love Him, because nobody loves Him."[21]

Confession and mercy have to be a pathway that guides us to our ultimate goal, which is Christ and sanctity through our merits in His merits. It is not only just a "thing" you do to be safe, it is a true sacrament of love and it has to allow us to love more, to draw love from the infinite love. This desire for mercy is an important, actually indispensable sacrament for our salvation, and moves us to be able to "love Him, love Jesus!" Sin is a rejection of Christ; we always have to think that. He loves you so much, don't you want to love Him? Don't you desire to receive that mercy, that is love?

• • •

Parents, teach your children how to love confession, because this is will make it easier for them. This allows them to start loving Christ at a younger age. Don't you desire everything that is good for your children? Don't you desire

---

[21] Armando Maggi, trans., *Maria Maddalena de`Pazzi: Selected Revelations* (New York: Paulist Press, 2000), 268.

the salvation of their souls? It is never too early to ask Christ for mercy, and children have such a pure heart, such a pure desire to love.

* * *

Confessors, blessed be your hands that can give that mercy! Love always the souls that are commended to you by Christ, they are a true gift for your soul and an open gate to the mercy of Christ. However, remember that they are like small children, they are seeking mercy, they desire love and true guidance. All this has to be done with Christ-like love and with a true desire for the salvation of souls, because this is not only a "human" task, it is a divine sacrament! That is why you are not a counselor or a psychologist. You are not just there to tell them what they want, but what they need and maybe, even what Christ desires from them. Love all of these souls and treasure them, give them time and mercy.

* * *

We are all sinners, searching for the love and mercy of Christ. Never judge a soul that searches for this mercy. We never know how much this soul is desired by Christ. It looks for mercy because Christ desires something from this soul. Love your neighbor and forgive him, even if it's difficult, and every time you get angry at him, confess it with your other sins. It will allow you to remember to love in the mercy of Christ.

* * *

Confession is not about "how holy we are," but how holy is Christ, who forgives and forgets. He who loves you and has so much mercy, who forgives and allows you to start again. If we learn to love the confessional, we will be open to the heart of Christ and we will be able to live "the path of mercy."

* * *

Avoid mortal sin, for the mercy of Christ, avoid that sin! It hurts Christ the most; however, if you tragically fall in one of them, do not be discouraged, because Lucifer wants you to fail. He wants you to be discouraged and give up, give up loving Christ. Never give up on a love that is so marvelous and so full of mercy. Our world is so full of sin because darkness is easier than light. Never be discouraged!

* * *

Dear confessors, never underestimate your task! Love your task! Listen to the souls, help them through the merciful eyes of Christ. Through your great example of sacrifice in the confessional, you might be that conversion for another "Saint Augustine." When you impose a penance, remember mercy and love, remember this soul just asked you for help to keep on following their path of holiness. Dear confessors, just try to love them as much as Christ loves you!

* * *

Be ever thankful for this marvelous sacrament, because it is a source of everlasting mercy!

Don't neglect it, rather love it. It is a pathway to heaven; it allows us to live in the mercy of Christ, especially in a world that desires mercy.

* * *

What are you waiting to confess? Don't think that before you die, you can ask for forgiveness, because not everyone has that grace. Don't you want to go to heaven? Don't you want to be with Jesus? He is waiting for you!

* * *

The Lord desires the salvation of all souls, not because all souls desire Him, even though many might think, "I am the one; I am the one that desires God." However, you are part of the cause that sent Him to die on the cross! Allow souls to go to Him, allow them to love Him, even if they are ungrateful, because He loves us, and in His infinite mercy, he continues to love us. He continues to give Himself fully, so that we might be one with Him.

* * *

Prayer and love, never forget them! They are the key to confession and they open the door to the mercy of our beloved Lord Jesus Christ!

* * *

Times of trial may come. Stay by the cross, which is ever steady, and allow Christ's mercy to cover you and to guide you, because He loves you! To desire mercy, to be thirsty for mercy in a world that is need of it, it's a huge step and once you receive it, you have to share it and become an apostle of mercy. Sometimes just a smile is an open gateway for Jesus to touch a soul. Open your heart to Jesus through mercy, so that you might be an open door for Him.

* * *

The spiritual ground on which we battle through before, during, and after confession has to be an opportunity to grow in a deeper relationship with Christ. It has to allow us to grow in grace.

Therefore, it is very important to avoid sin. Sin creates tension in ourselves and "weakens" our relationship with Christ. However, always remember that the confessional is an open opportunity to embrace Jesus and in this way, to also regain your strength and courage in Him.

* * *

O Love! Oh, merciful Love! How come I cannot love you like you love me? O Love, O Love, there is a fire in your heart that burns constantly in love for all sinners and extends through forgiveness. Why can they not see it? Why can I not love you, the way you love them? Oh, have mercy on me, Lord! O Love, my Love! Teach me to love through mercy, through that fire that is everlasting for my neighbor, who lives the consequences of my sins, of my anger or negligence. O Love, teach me to love them and forgive them, in the way you have forgiven me! O Love, my eternal merciful Love! Teach me to trust, teach me to trust in thy mercy, because, my Love, I cannot trust myself, let alone my neighbor. If you teach me to trust you, then I will be able to love without measures, as your merciful heart does! Oh Love, have mercy on me!

CONCLUSION

Many may wonder, Why is it so necessary? Why is mercy necessary? Don't we live in a world that has it "all"? Isn't the human society doing great? Isn't mercy for those who are poor or needy?

You may surprise yourself, but under the pretty mask of the "world" there is a lack of God, a lack of His love, and that love is truly mercy. Mercy moves God, it allows Him to forgive our lack of love and charity, but even more, it allows Him to keep on working in us through grace, because we give up on God, but God never gives up on us. However, remember as well that your heart in which He lives, He cannot co-habit with sin and with the devil. That is why the longer you avoid confession, the easier does sin become. We must love Jesus so much, so much that every sin will become horrible to ourselves, for our need for mercy strengthens us to trust in Him. He gives Himself to us and we should give ourselves to Him, work on our daily sanctification, and trust in His Merciful Heart. His loving Heart is everlasting and is truly ever giving, God loves you! Never forget that!

Bibliography

"A Few Thoughts: Go to Confession." Mother Angelica Live Classics. Published on 9 August 2011. Accessed 10 April 2017, https://www.youtube.com/watch?v=-o4O-_TqgWk.

Angelica, Mother M. "Why Do You Stay Away?" EWTN. Accessed 22 May 2017, https://www.ewtn.com/library/mother/ma53.htm.

Brown, Hilda. *She Shall Crush Thy Head: Selected Writings of St. Maximilian Kolbe*. Phoenix, Arizona: Leonine Publishers, 2015.

Brown, R., trans. and ed. *The Little Flowers of St. Francis*. Garden City, New York: Double Day & Company, Inc., 1958.

Catechism of the Catholic Church "The Sacrament of Penance and Reconciliation." Accessed 10 April 2017, http://www.vatican.va/archive/ccc_css/archive/catechism/p2s2c2a4.htm.

"El Papa: Oración no es magia y no rezamos a un 'Dios cósmico' sino a un Padre cercano." Aciprensa. Published on 20 June 2013. Accessed 11 April 2017, https://www.aciprensa.com/noticias/el-papa-oracion-no-es-magia-y-no-rezamos-a-un-dios-cosmico-sino-a-un-padre-cercano-82149/.

Francis, Pope. *Lent with Pope Francis*. Edited by Donna Giaimo. Boston, MA: Pauline Books & Media, 2014.

Ignatius of Loyola. *Ejercicios Espirituales*. Santander: Editorial Sal Terrae, 2013.

John Paul II, Pope. "Analysis of Knowledge and of Procreation." L`Osservatore Romano. Accessed 9 March 2017, https://www.ewtn.com/library/PAPALDOC/jp2tb19.htm.

Lucia of Fatima, Sister. *Memorias de la Hermana Lucia,* 14th ed. Edited by Louis Kondor. Fátima: Fundação Francisco e Jacinta Marto, 2016.

Maggi, Armando, trans. *Maria Maddalena de`Pazzi: Selected Revelations.* New York: Paulist Press, 2000.

Maravillas de Jesús. *Pensamientos Maravillas de Jesús.* Èditions du Signe, 2002.

de Montfort, Saint Louis-Marie. *True Devotion to Mary.* Montfort Missionaries. Accessed 14 March 2019, http://montfort.org/content/uploads/pdf/PDF_ES_26_1.pdf.

Solano, J. *Desarrollo Histórico de la Reparación en el culto al Corazón de Jesús.* Roma: Centro Cuore di Cristo, 1980.

_____. *Conocer al Corazón de Jesús, Pensamientos y Pistas de Búsqueda.* Centro Cuore di Cristo, 1982.

About the Author

Christopher Lopez is an active young Catholic from Guatemala. He has lived in Tromsø, Norway, for more than seven years. Lopez pulls joy from the practice of his Catholic faith. He especially has a strong desire to provide testimony on the Sacrament of Penance and the importance of engaging in sacramental confession frequently.

About Leonine Publishers

Leonine Publishers LLC makes fine Catholic literature available to Catholics throughout the English-speaking world. Leonine Publishers offers an innovative "hybrid" approach to book publication that helps authors as well as readers. Please visit our web site at www.leoninepublishers.com to learn more about us. Browse our online bookstore to find more solid Catholic titles to uplift, challenge, and inspire.

Our patron and namesake is Pope Leo XIII, a prudent, yet uncompromising pope during the stormy years at the close of the 19th century. Please join us as we ask his intercession for our family of readers and authors.

www.leoninepublishers.com